WISCONSIN

WISCONSIN

HELLO
U.S.A.

by Gretchen Bratvold

 Lerner Publications Company

You'll find this picture of a Holstein cow's coat at the beginning of each chapter. Many of the 1.3 million dairy cows in Wisconsin are Holsteins. Holsteins produce milk for the ice cream, butter, and other dairy products made in Wisconsin. No two Holsteins have the same pattern of spots.

Cover (left): Dairy farm near Tigerton, Wisconsin. Cover (right): Green Bay Packers quarterback Brett Favre during a game against the Arizona Cardinals. Pages 2-3: American Birkebeiner ski race, Hayward, Wisconsin. Page 3: State capitol in Madison.

This book is available in two editions:
Library binding by Lerner Publications Company, a division of Lerner Publishing Group
Soft cover by First Avenue Editions, an imprint of Lerner Publishing Group
241 First Avenue North
Minneapolis, MN 55401 U.S.A.

Website address: www.lernerbooks.com

Library of Congress Cataloging-in-Publication Data

Bratvold, Gretchen, 1959–
    Wisconsin / Gretchen Bratvold. (Revised and expanded 2nd edition)
        p.   cm. — (Hello U.S.A.)
    Includes index.
    ISBN: 0–8225–4052–5 (lib. bdg. : alk. paper)
    ISBN: 0–8225–4156–4 (pbk.)
    1. Wisconsin—Juvenile literature. [1. Wisconsin.] I. Title. II. Series.
    F581.3.B73 2002
    977.5—dc21   00–140184

Manufactured in the United States of America
1 2 3 4 5 6 – JR – 07 06 05 04 03 02

CONTENTS

Snowy winters bring a chill to the forests and farmland of southwestern Wisconsin *(above)*.
Wisconsinites head to their state's lakes for sailboating *(facing page)* in the summer.

THE LAND

America's Dairyland

With hundreds of dairy farms, Wisconsin is well known for its milk, butter, and cheese. For this reason, Wisconsin's rolling hills, fertile plains and valleys, and thousands of lakes have come to be called America's Dairyland.

Wisconsin is located in the upper midwestern area of the United States. The state has four neighbors— Michigan, Illinois, Iowa, and Minnesota. The Mississippi River runs along much of the western border. Two huge lakes, Superior and Michigan, also form part of Wisconsin's boundaries. These bodies of water belong to the five Great Lakes of North America.

The drawing of Wisconsin on this page is called a political map. It shows features created by people, including cities, railways, and parks. The map on the facing page is called a physical map. It shows physical features of Wisconsin, such as coasts, islands, mountains, rivers, and lakes. The colors represent a range of elevations, or heights above sea level (see legend box).

This map also shows the geographical regions of Wisconsin.

Superior

Bayfield

Chequamegon National Forest

Hayward

Chequamegon National Forest

Nicolet National Forest

Crandon

Peshtigo

Seymour

Green Bay

Appleton

Two Rivers

Oshkosh

Ripon

Fond du Lac

La Crosse

Wisconsin Dells

Baraboo

Spring Green

Watertown

Prairie du Chien

Blue Mounds

Mount Horeb

★ **Madison**

Milwaukee

Dodgeville

Eagle

Racine

Kenosha

WISCONSIN
Political Map

★ State capital

0   20   40 Miles

0   20   40   60   80 Kilometers

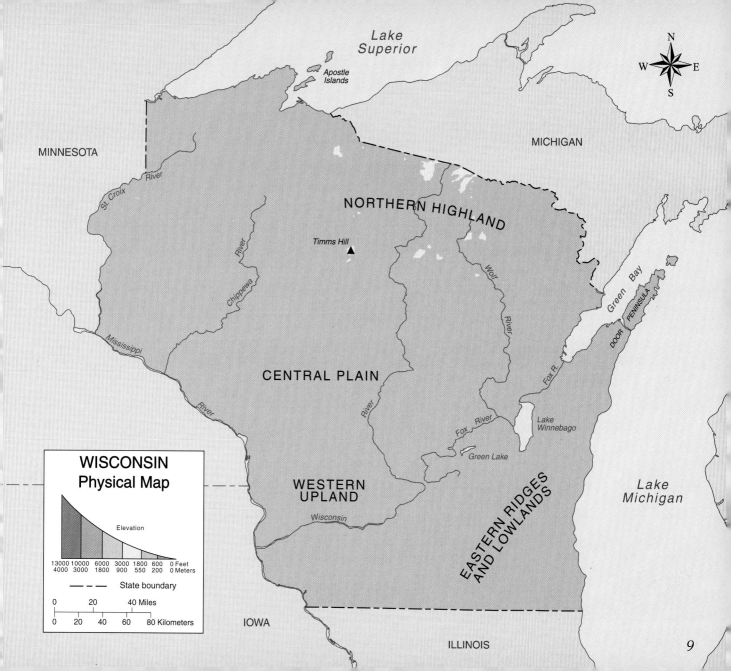

Lake Superior

Apostle Islands

MINNESOTA

St. Croix River

River

Chippewa

Mississippi

River

MICHIGAN

NORTHERN HIGHLAND

Timms Hill ▲

Wolf

River

Green Bay

DOOR PENINSULA

CENTRAL PLAIN

Fox R.

Fox River

Lake Winnebago

Green Lake

WESTERN UPLAND

Wisconsin

EASTERN RIDGES AND LOWLANDS

Lake Michigan

N
W   E
S

WISCONSIN
Physical Map

Elevation

| 13000 | 10000 | 6000 | 3000 | 1800 | 600 | 0 Feet |
| 4000 | 3000 | 1800 | 900 | 550 | 200 | 0 Meters |

State boundary

0   20   40 Miles

0   20   40   60   80 Kilometers

IOWA

ILLINOIS

9

Seventy-thousand years ago, during the **Ice Age**, enormous sheets of ice called **glaciers** covered a large part of North America. As the glaciers inched their way through the Great Lakes region, they ground away soil and rocks and shaped the land that would later be called Wisconsin.

The state has four main land regions, and glaciers carved three of them—the Northern Highland, the Central Plain, and the Eastern Ridges and Lowlands. The fourth region, the Western Upland, was untouched by the glaciers.

Lake Superior's shore is dotted with rocks and boulders that were left behind by glaciers.

Swimmers plunge into the Wisconsin River from sandstone cliffs in the Wisconsin Dells.

The Northern Highland expands across most of northern Wisconsin. Glaciers in this region hollowed out basins that later filled with water. They also left behind mounds of earth and stones. These rocky hills are called **moraines.** The state's highest point, Timms Hill, rises to 1,952 feet in the Northern Highland.

South of the highland region lies the Central Plain, which has both level and hilly land. Low, flat terrain stretches across the southern end of the Central Plain. Thousands of years ago, water covered this part of the region.

The Eastern Ridges and Lowlands spread across much of eastern Wisconsin. Rich deposits of earth left behind by the glaciers make this gently rolling region the most fertile in the state.

Glaciers did not pass through Wisconsin's fourth region. For this reason, the Western Upland has more rugged terrain than other areas of the state. Limestone and sandstone **bluffs** rise from the banks of the Mississippi River in the southwestern corner of the region.

Crops such as corn grow well on the gently rolling land of the Eastern Ridges and Lowlands.

Wisconsin's many lakes provide
nesting sites for loons and
other birds.

Wisconsin has many rivers. In the western half of the state, the Wisconsin, Chippewa, and Saint Croix Rivers flow into the great Mississippi. In the east, the Wolf and Fox Rivers and many smaller streams empty into Lake Michigan. Hundreds of waterfalls spill over steep drops along these rivers.

Long ago, water from melting glaciers collected in the hollows the ice had gouged out of the earth. As a result, Wisconsin has more than 13,000 natural lakes, mostly in the north. Green Lake is the deepest, and Lake Winnebago is the largest.

Many Wisconsinites enjoy winter sports like skiing.

For most of Wisconsin, summer temperatures average about 70° F. The far north, however, is about 10° F cooler. Winters are often long and cold throughout the state, with temperatures sometimes plunging far below 0° F in the northwest. Along the shores of Lakes Superior and Michigan, breezes from the water warm the air in the winter and cool it in the summer.

Because plenty of rain and snow fall in Wisconsin, the state has lush plant life during the warmer months. Thunderstorms and occasional tornadoes pass through the region in the spring and summer.

Forests shade much of the northern half of Wisconsin. But many open fields stretch across the south. Early settlers cleared the trees from this area so they could farm the rich soil. Wildflowers and shrubs such as blueberry, Juneberry, and huckleberry also grow in Wisconsin.

Wisconsin's state flower is the wood violet *(above right)*. A young white-tailed deer rests in the woods *(above left)*.

Many white-tailed deer scamper through Wisconsin's forests, where black bears, coyotes, and foxes also roam. Excellent swimmers, Wisconsin's beavers and muskrats splash in the state's rivers and lakes. Skunks and badgers burrow underground.

The badger, Wisconsin's state animal, uses long claws to tunnel through the ground.

Pioneers and Progressives

 uring the Ice Age, a strip of land connected the North American and Asian continents at the Bering Strait. Hunters from Asia followed herds of animals across this long bridge of land and entered America. By 6000 B.C., Asians had settled in various parts of North and South America. These people and their descendants are called Indians, or Native Americans.

Viburnum berries in early winter

Early Routes from Asia into North America

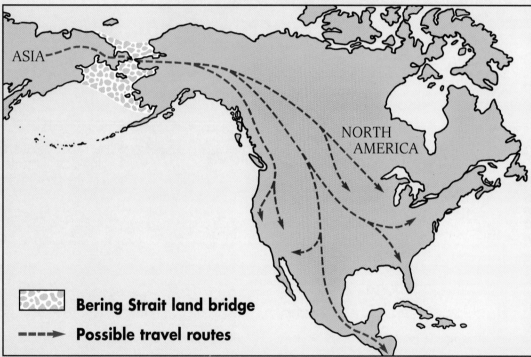

ASIA

NORTH AMERICA

Bering Strait land bridge

---▶ Possible travel routes

During the Ice Age, North America and Asia were connected by a small strip of land at what later became the Bering Strait. According to many scientists, North America's first Indians traveled across the Bering Strait land bridge from Asia more than 40,000 years ago. They spread out all over North America. Some of them eventually settled in what later became Wisconsin.

Torchlights helped the Menominee Indians spear fish at night. The bright flames attracted fish to the surface of the water.

The Indians who moved into Wisconsin came sometime after 10,000 B.C., when the last glaciers in the area had melted. Some of the newcomers were the Winnebago, Dakota, and Menominee.

The Indians hunted and fished, and they grew corn, beans, and squash. Some of them went out in canoes to gather wild rice, which grew in shallow water. They used bark and brush to build homes, and they buried their dead in large mounds of earth shaped like birds, bears, and other animals.

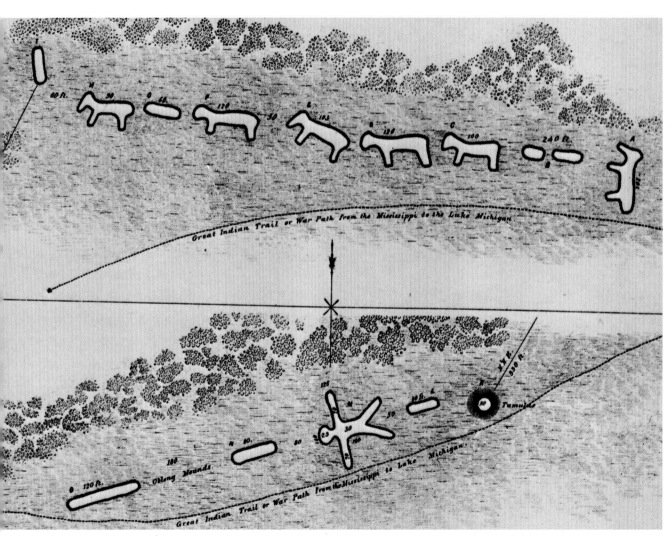

Hundreds of years ago, the Indians of Wisconsin buried their dead in huge, animal-shaped mounds. Some of the mounds were more than 100 feet long.

In the 1600s, many other Indian groups—including the Sauk, Fox, Kickapoo, Ojibway, and Potawatomi—arrived in Wisconsin from the east. Some came to escape unfriendly Europeans who had settled along the East Coast. Other groups sought safety from warring Indians.

The first Europeans to set foot in Wisconsin probably arrived around the 1620s. Coming from eastern Canada, the French explorer Jean Nicolet sailed through the Great Lakes and landed on the shore of Green Bay in 1634. There he met the Winnebago Indians who lived along the bay.

At first Nicolet thought he had found a water route to China. With his beard and white skin, Nicolet looked very strange to the Native Americans who greeted him.

In late summer, Ojibway Indians harvested rice growing in shallow lake water.

Nicolet was surprised to find Indians when he had expected Chinese people. Disappointed, he returned to his home in Canada. He had learned what the Native Americans already knew—North America was a huge chunk of land.

Jean Nicolet thought he had landed in China when he arrived in Wisconsin in 1634. He wore a Chinese robe when he greeted the Native Americans.

More French people—especially Roman Catholic **missionaries** and fur traders—came from Canada in the mid-1600s. In 1673 Father Jacques Marquette and Louis Jolliet, a fur trader, explored the Fox and Wisconsin Rivers on their way to the Mississippi River. Marquette and Jolliet were the first Europeans to explore the Mississippi as far south as the mouth of the Arkansas River.

French missionaries like Marquette wanted to teach the Indians the Christian religion. The fur traders depended on the hunting skills of the Indians, who were experts at trapping and skinning animals.

For their work, the Indians received European goods such as mirrors, knives, guns, iron pots, glassware, and alcohol. Beaver coats and hats were fashionable in Europe, so beaver pelts sold for high prices.

Gradually, the Indians became more dependent on the goods they got from the fur traders. The traders then made the Indians bring in more and more pelts to trade for the items they wanted.

The Catholic Church sent Father Jacques Marquette to work as a missionary in French territory in North America.

Boatmen called voyageurs carried furs and other trade goods between Indian and French settlements during the 1700s. After paddling all day, the voyageurs camped along rocky shores.

For many decades, the Indians and French lived together peacefully. Eventually, however, trouble arose over control of the Fox and Wisconsin Rivers. The Fox Indians and the French relied on these waterways for travel. In 1712 war erupted. Battles continued for 28 years, until the French overpowered the Fox.

The war made the other Indian groups besides the Fox angry with the French. Without the support of these Indians, French strength in the region weakened. Between 1754 and 1763, during the French and Indian War, the French fought against the British for North American territory. Some Indians sided with the French in this war. But the British defeated the French, and Wisconsin passed to British control.

British rule did not last long, however. After Britain lost the American Revolution (1775–1783), Wisconsin became part of the territory of the United States. By this time, many of the Indians in Wisconsin had died. Many had been killed in battles during the 1700s, and others had caught deadly diseases from the European newcomers.

To find lead near the earth's surface, Wisconsin's early miners dug into the sides of hills.

In the 1820s, more white people began moving into southwestern Wisconsin because it had rich deposits of lead. These settlers built permanent towns and mined the lead, which was needed to make paint and other products.

As the demand for lead increased, many miners came to Wisconsin. Some of the miners lived in caves that they dug into the hillsides. These people were called "Badgers," because, like the animal, they burrowed shelters into the earth. Eventually, Badger became a nickname for all Wisconsinites.

In 1832 a Sauk Indian chief named Black Hawk led 1,000 Indians across the Mississippi River from Iowa into Illinois to regain farmland taken over by the white settlers. Thinking that the Indians were going to war, the settlers called out their troops. The Indians fled to Wisconsin and fought back, but they were greatly outnumbered. Nearly all of Black Hawk's people were killed.

After the Black Hawk War, there were no more Indian wars in Wisconsin. U.S. officials made the Indians sign **treaties** giving up control of their territory.

Black Hawk and his followers clashed with U.S. troops at the Battle of Bad Axe in 1832. As Black Hawk's followers tried to surrender, U.S. troops killed almost 300 of them.

Indians were forced to give their land in southwestern Wisconsin to the U.S. government at this meeting at Prairie du Chien in 1825.

By 1848 the United States had gotten legal claim to all of the land in the region. That same year, Wisconsin became the 30th state to join the Union.

Many more white settlers moved to Wisconsin in the mid-1800s. Between 1835 and 1850, the population grew from 11,000 to well over 300,000. Lumberjacks chopped down the forests, and farmers cleared away the tree stumps and planted crops. In the second half of the 1800s, Germans, Norwegians, and Poles came from Europe and Canada. The arrival of these newcomers, called **immigrants,** caused the population to quickly pass 1 million.

Settlement of Wisconsin's Largest Immigrant Groups

Southern and eastern Wisconsin were the first areas in the state to be settled by immigrants. The earliest newcomers came from Britain and Germany in the mid-1800s. Norwegians, Swedes, and Danes followed soon after, but most of them made their homes in western Wisconsin. By 1920 Finns joined the ethnic mix and settled in the north. By far the greatest number of immigrants came from Germany.

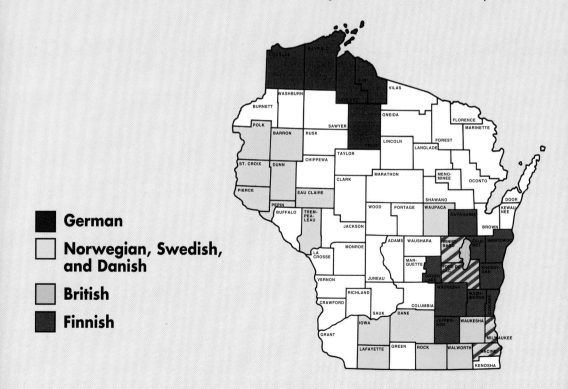

- **German**
- **Norwegian, Swedish, and Danish**
- **British**
- **Finnish**

Many of Wisconsin's immigrants worked as lumberjacks in the state's northern forests. They worked mostly in late fall and winter. These lumberjacks use a two-person crosscut saw to cut down a tree.

Immigrants moved to places in Wisconsin where others from the same country had already settled. Life for the immigrants was easier when their neighbors shared the same language, religion, and customs. As more people from other countries arrived and settled in separate areas, Wisconsin became a patchwork of many ethnic groups.

The immigrants brought new skills to the region, and some found new ways to make a living. Farmers started raising dairy cattle instead of growing wheat, and milk production and cheese-making began. Many factories sprang up in the cities along Lake Michigan. Railroads expanded, breweries opened, and paper mills were built.

By the 1890s, some of the state's political leaders were thinking about how the government could improve the lives of Wisconsinites. For several decades, the Republican Party had controlled the government. But many important Republicans used their power unfairly, carefully protecting their own interests in the state's successful lumber and railroad businesses.

The Peshtigo Fire

On the night of October 8, 1871, the worst fire in Wisconsin's history swept through Peshtigo, killing about 1,000 people. Hundreds of residents jumped into the Peshtigo River for protection. But danger was everywhere. In the river, they had to struggle to keep afloat in water full of people, horses, and cattle.

On the same night, another blaze raged through Chicago in the neighboring state of Illinois, killing only about 200 people. But the Chicago fire got all the attention in the country's newspapers. Few people heard of the Peshtigo fire until the next day, when it was too late to help.

Some Wisconsinites were unhappy with the government of Wisconsin. They decided to split away from the Republicans and form their own branch within the Republican Party.

Headed by a man named Robert M. La Follette Sr., the new program was called **Progressivism.** It followed progressive, or new, ideas. The Progressives wanted to give more power to the people. They thought all Wisconsinites—not just a few— should have a say in how the economy and the government worked.

In 1900 La Follette, nick-named "Fighting Bob," was elected **governor** of Wisconsin. La Follette and the Progressives guided the state through many important changes. For example, new state laws required factory owners to make their companies safer places to work.

Robert M. La Follette Sr. gives a captivating speech at a county fair in 1897.

If a worker got hurt on the job, the company had to pay the doctor's fees. Other laws kept the price of railroad tickets from increasing too rapidly.

Fighting Bob went to Washington, D.C., for 19 years to represent Wisconsin as a **senator** in the U.S. Congress. In 1924 La Follette ran for president of the country as the Progressive Party candidate, but he lost the election. Support for the Progressives declined after La Follette's death in 1925.

Belle Case La Follette speaks to farmers and their families. Mrs. La Follette, wife of Robert M. La Follette, worked to gain women the right to vote.

During the late 1800s and early 1900s, railroads transported people and goods to cities and towns all over Wisconsin.

The 1930s were hard for people all over the country. Known as the Great Depression, this period left many people short of money, food, and other necessities. Wisconsinites turned once again to the Progressive Party to solve their problems.

During the depression, La Follette's son Philip served as governor of Wisconsin. The younger La Follette tried to fix some of the state's problems by giving factory workers more power in the workplace and by helping farmers pay their bills. Philip also helped support people who had lost their jobs. He created new jobs by starting projects such as the building of roads.

Wisconsin's Progressive Party died out in 1946, when Joseph McCarthy, a Republican, won the state's election for U.S. senator. McCarthy was concerned that **Communists** were beginning to fill government jobs. His followers called him a patriot, but others said he falsely accused workers of disloyalty to the United States. In the end, McCarthy was not able to prove his charges.

Since the McCarthy Era, Wisconsinites who believe in Progressive ideals have usually joined the Democratic Party, and the state government has shifted between Democratic and Republican control.

During the 1980s and early 1990s, some of Wisconsin's traditional industries experienced a decline. The value of farmland dropped, and the number of Wisconsin's farms decreased. In addition, several of the breweries that once made Milwaukee famous either closed or left the city. But by the late 1990s, the economy was booming. Jobs in manufacturing and high-tech industries became available for many Wisconsinites.

Wisconsin's state capitol, located in Madison, has been the site of many historic and progressive decisions.

Republican Tommy Thompson served as governor of Wisconsin from 1987 until 2001, when he became secretary of the Department of Health and Human Services under President George W. Bush. During Thompson's years in office, Wisconsin became a leader in welfare reform. Welfare is money or help given to poor people by the government. In reforming its welfare system, the state government has changed the way it helps low-income families. People learn new skills to get the jobs they need to support themselves and their families. Wisconsin has also worked to improve public education in the state. Wisconsinites continue to lead the way in improving life for their fellow citizens.

PEOPLE & ECONOMY

Badgers at Work and Play

ince the arrival of the first Europeans, Wisconsin's population has shifted from being nearly all Indian to nearly all white. Most modern Wisconsinites were born in the United States, but their ancestors came from many lands. People from Britain, Germany, Scandinavia, Italy, and eastern Europe settled in Wisconsin during the 1800s and early 1900s.

Blacks, who make up about 5 percent of the state's population, have come to Wisconsin primarily since the 1940s. More recently, Latinos and Asians have moved to the state.

Academy Award–winning actor Ernest Borgnine serves as Grand Clown every year in Milwaukee's Great Circus Parade.

A race curves down a street on a sunny day in Milwaukee.

Of Wisconsin's 5.4 million people, fewer than 1 percent—about 45,000—are Native Americans. Many of the Indians live on **reservations**—areas of land that are reserved for a specific tribe. Residents of the reservations have their own government and enforce their own laws.

Two-thirds of the state's population live in cities. About half of these city-dwellers live in Milwaukee, Wisconsin's largest city. Most big communities—including Milwaukee, Madison (the capital), Green Bay, Kenosha, and Appleton—are located in the southern half of the state.

Milwaukee and Madison are the main cultural centers in Wisconsin. Orchestras, ballets, theater groups, and many museums attract both Wisconsinites and visitors. Students also take field trips to museums that specialize in ships, railroads, and circuses, as well as in art, history, and natural science.

Many of the buildings in Milwaukee and other places are like museums. Their architecture—the style in which they are built—tells us about the history of the state. Some of these buildings, like Taliesin, near Spring Green, and the headquarters of the S. C. Johnson and Son Company in Racine, were designed in the early 1900s by Frank Lloyd Wright. Wright was one of the most famous designers of buildings in the United States.

A sixth-grade teacher helps his students with textbook exercises.

Wisconsin began offering free education in 1845, when its first public elementary school opened. A public high school began operating four years later. In 1856 Margaretha Schurz set up the first kindergarten in the United States in Watertown, Wisconsin.

The Green Bay Packers attract loyal and enthusiastic fans.

    With three professional athletic teams, Wisconsin is a great state for sports fans. Thousands of Wisconsinites cheer for the Green Bay Packers during the football season. Wisconsin's baseball team is the Milwaukee Brewers, and the Milwaukee Bucks play basketball. In addition, Wisconsin hosts auto races and the American Birkebeiner cross-country ski race.

Every February, thousands of cross-country skiers come to Hayward to participate in the American Birkebeiner, North America's largest ski race.

A machine winds paper into huge rolls at a Wisconsin paper mill.

Nearly one-fourth of all Wisconsinites work in factories. Workers in Milwaukee and other cities in the southeast make equipment such as engines, tractors, bulldozers, and power cranes.

The forests of Wisconsin supply a large paper industry, and many people in the lower Fox River valley and the upper Wisconsin River valley work in paper mills. In fact, Wisconsinites make about 11 percent of the paper used in the United States. The mills also produce paper boxes, tissue paper, and cardboard.

Food processing jobs—such as making dairy products, canning fruits and vegetables, brewing beer, and packing meat—are also important in Wisconsin. Many of the state's food products are sold in other states.

Beer brews in huge kettles at one of Wisconsin's breweries *(left)*. Apples *(below)* grow on some of Wisconsin's farms.

Most of the money earned in Wisconsin comes from service jobs. This type of work includes jobs in banking, schools, and restaurants. Government workers earn about 11 percent of Wisconsin's yearly income. Only 2 percent of all the money earned in the state comes from farming. But when all 50 states are ranked according to yearly income from agriculture, Wisconsin is usually among the top 10.

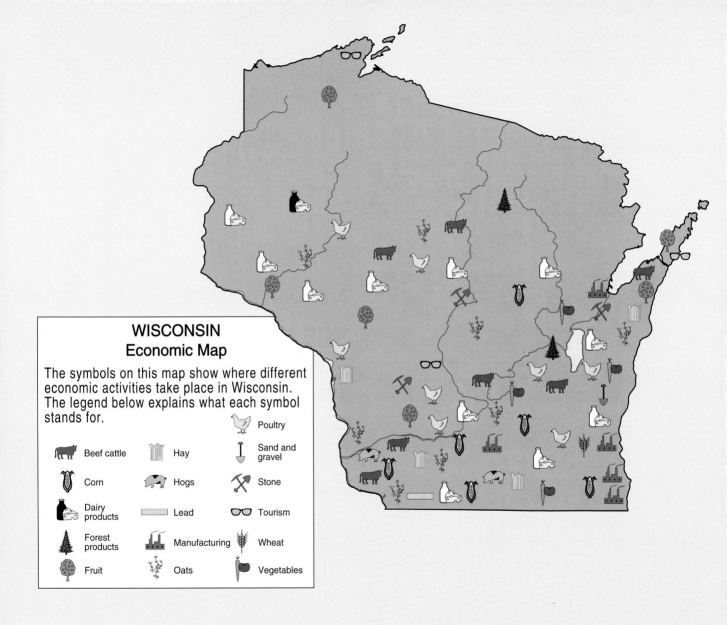

WISCONSIN
Economic Map

The symbols on this map show where different economic activities take place in Wisconsin. The legend below explains what each symbol stands for.

Beef cattle		Hay		Sand and gravel	
Corn		Hogs		Stone	
Dairy products		Lead		Tourism	
Forest products		Manufacturing		Wheat	
Fruit		Oats		Vegetables	

Most of the state's farms are located in the south and the east—areas that have the richest soil and the longest growing season. Dairying is the most important type of farming. Nicknamed America's Dairyland, Wisconsin produces more milk than almost any other state in the country. Some of the milk is processed into butter, cheese, or ice cream at plants throughout the state.

Along the roadsides, signs advertise "Cheese" and "Cheese Curds" for sale at local stores and restaurants. No wonder, since Wisconsin makes about one-third of the cheese produced in the country. The state also produces one-fourth of the nation's butter.

Some farmers raise beef cattle, hogs, and chickens. These animals are sold to meat-packing plants in Milwaukee, Madison, and Green Bay. There they are butchered and then packaged for market.

A young girl cuddles one of her family's dairy calves.

Throughout the state, farmers grow hay, corn, and oats to feed livestock.

Most of the vegetable crops—including peas, beets, beans, cabbages, cucumbers, potatoes, and sweet corn—are sent to factories for canning. Some farmers grow fruits such as cranberries, strawberries, raspberries, and apples.

People from other states travel to Wisconsin year-round to enjoy the state's natural beauty. Skiing, hiking, fishing, and swimming are a few of the popular outdoor activities that vacationers like. The money these tourists spend adds to Wisconsin's earnings.

September is harvesttime for cranberries.

Mining and fishing were once big businesses in Wisconsin, but today they bring in only a small amount of the state's total earnings. Wisconsin's miners dig sand, gravel, stone, and lime for use in construction. Those who make their living from fishing operate mostly on Lake Michigan.

The leaves on Wisconsin's trees turn vivid colors in the fall *(left)*. A child fishes on one of Wisconsin's lakes *(above)*.

In Green Bay's harbor, a ship's lights sparkle in the night.

Superior, Milwaukee, and Green Bay are busy port cities on the Great Lakes. The harbors receive many products, including coal, which is used to create electricity for homes and businesses around the state. And from these ports, dairy products, grain, machinery, and other goods made in Wisconsin are shipped throughout the country and overseas.

THE ENVIRONMENT

Keeping Wisconsin Clean

With abundant soil, water, timber, fish, and wildlife, Wisconsin has a wealth of natural resources. Special care must be taken of these treasures, however, if they are to last. One natural resource that many Wisconsinites are concerned about is **groundwater**—the water below the surface of the earth. Pollution has already made some of the state's surface water (lakes and rivers) unsafe to drink.

Wisconsin's beautiful forests and waterways are becoming polluted.

Wisconsinites must face the challenge of cleaning up polluted streams in their state.

Most of Wisconsin's supply of drinking water comes from groundwater, but this water supply can also become polluted. Farmers spray pesticides on their fields to control insects, weeds, and other pests. They use fertilizers to make crops grow better. Many of these chemicals are very powerful and can harm the environment. Eventually, they may seep through the soil and pollute groundwater.

Wisconsin's paper mills and other factories cause air pollution, which eventually contaminates land and water.

Possible Sources of Groundwater Pollution

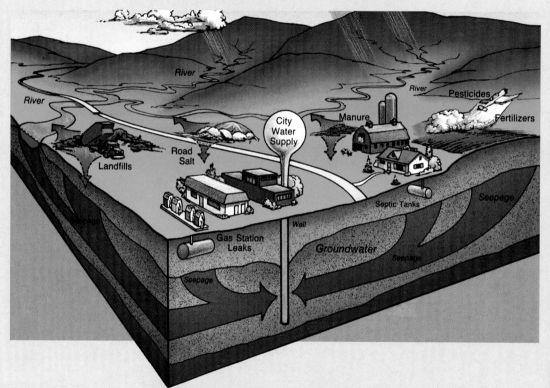

In Wisconsin and other states, a variety of chemicals can pollute the groundwater. These include chemicals used to make crops grow, salt used on icy roads, and gasoline. This diagram shows ways that those chemicals and other substances can seep into the ground and pollute the groundwater.

A specific threat to groundwater in Wisconsin is a proposed zinc and copper ore mine near Crandon. If the mine is built, groundwater would be removed from the mine area. When the mine is no longer in use, large amounts of groundwater would seep back into the mine and become polluted by its minerals. Some people worry that the polluted groundwater will seep into nearby rivers and streams. Scientists must find ways to treat and dispose of the polluted water without harming the rivers near the mine.

Some environmentalists worry that the Wolf River may become polluted if the Crandon mine is developed. The Wolf River is home to fish and many other kinds of wildlife that may be threatened by poisons from the mine.

To help keep their landfills from overflowing, as this one has, Wisconsinites try to throw away less trash each day.

Another environmental problem in Wisconsin is the large amount of garbage people toss out each day. Wisconsin's landfills (places where trash is buried) are filling up. Most will be full by the year 2006. Unless people start to produce less waste, Wisconsin will have to create more landfills.

Cutting down on the amount of trash thrown away is one way to protect the environment. The Wisconsin Department of Natural Resources (DNR) encourages people to buy items that have less packaging and to reuse things until they are worn out. Some materials, such as plastic and rubber, are so tough that they do not break down even after they are thrown away.

Another way to protect the environment and conserve space in Wisconsin's landfills is to recycle. Recycling is the collection and reprocessing of materials for reuse. Paper, glass jars, metal cans, plastic containers, tires, and oil are some of the products that Wisconsin recycles.

Wisconsinites of all ages do their part in their state's recycling efforts.

Each person in the state can participate in the recycling program by separating articles that can be recycled from the rest of his or her garbage. In fact, 1.4 million tons of waste from Wisconsin cities were recycled in 1998.

Wisconsin has made laws to protect the environment against waste from factories. Some company owners, however, do not want to change. Updated

Wisconsinites preserve their state's natural beauty by protecting the environment.

equipment creates less pollution, but it also costs a lot of money. And some business leaders say that the waste their companies create is not really that dangerous. Other factory owners are more willing to cooperate and have already followed the new laws. If citizens and companies in Wisconsin try to help protect the environment, the state can be a clean, healthy place to live.

Fun Facts

The name Wisconsin may mean "gathering of the waters" or "place of the beaver." The word comes from the French version of an Ojibway Indian term.

The famous Ringling Brothers Circus first performed in Baraboo, Wisconsin, in 1884. The company still tours the country, and its posters, wagons, and equipment are displayed at Circus World Museum in Baraboo.

The Republican Party was started at an antislavery meeting in Ripon, Wisconsin, in 1854.

A Wisconsin paper manufacturer invented and sold the world's first facial tissues in 1917. The product was advertised as an easy, disposable way to wipe off makeup. Imagine the company's surprise when it learned that its customers were using the tissues, called Kleenex, to blow their noses!

On August 5, 1989, "the biggest hamburger in the world" was made in Seymour, Wisconsin. It weighed 2.5 tons and served 13,000 visitors. Seymour claims that it's the place where the hamburger was invented. In 1885 Charlie Nagreen started selling hamburgers at the Outagamie County Fair in Seymour.

Wisconsin's dairy cows produce 2.6 billion gallons of milk each year. That amount would be enough to fill more than 8 nine-foot-deep Olympic-size swimming pools every day!

STATE SONG

"On, Wisconsin" was originally written by William T. Purdy and Carl Beck in 1909 for the University of Wisconsin football team. In 1913 J. S. Hubbard and Charles D. Rosa wrote new lyrics for the song. "On, Wisconsin" became the state's official song in 1959.

ON, WISCONSIN

Words by J. S. Hubbard and Charles D. Rosa
Music by William T. Purdy

You can hear "On, Wisconsin" by visiting this website:
<http://www.laurasmidiheaven.com/statesongs-W.html>

A WISCONSIN RECIPE

In America's Dairyland, people enjoy eating and making all kinds of dairy products, including ice cream. In fact, Two Rivers, Wisconsin, calls itself the home of the ice cream sundae. With the recipe below, you can make ice cream at home—and you don't need an ice cream maker. You can even make your own ice cream sundae.

EASY HOMEMADE ICE CREAM

You will need:

½ cup cold milk
1 can (14 ounces) sweetened condensed milk
1 pint heavy whipping cream

1 tablespoon vanilla extract
⅛ teaspoon salt

1. In medium bowl, stir together milk, vanilla, condensed milk, and salt. Set aside.
2. In large bowl, beat heavy cream with an electric mixer until stiff peaks form.
3. Gently fold milk mixture into whipped cream.
4. Pour into shallow 2-quart dish, cover, and freeze for 4 hours. Stir once after 2 hours or when edges start to harden.
5. Remove dish from freezer. You can eat the ice cream right away, or, if you want, you can make a sundae. Sprinkle chocolate chips or chopped nuts on your ice cream. Add whipped cream or chocolate sauce. Enjoy your ice cream sundae!

Makes 3 pints.

HISTORICAL TIMELINE

10,000 B.C.   Indians begin moving into Wisconsin.

A.D. 1600   Sauk, Fox, Kickapoo, Ojibway, and Potawatomi Indians arrive from eastern North America.

1634   Jean Nicolet lands at Green Bay.

1673   French explorers Father Jacques Marquette and Louis Jolliet travel Wisconsin rivers.

1740   The French defeat the Fox Indians after 28 years of fighting.

1763   Wisconsin becomes part of British territory after the French and Indian War.

1783   The American Revolution ends; Wisconsin is added to U.S. territory.

1820   Lead mining begins in southwestern Wisconsin.

1832   Black Hawk and his followers unsuccessfully try to win their land back from white settlers during the Black Hawk War.

1848   Wisconsin becomes the 30th state.

1850 The population of Wisconsin reaches 300,000.

1851 The first railroad in Wisconsin is built.

1854 The Republican Party is founded in Ripon, Wisconsin.

1856 Margaretha Schurz sets up the first kindergarten in the United States.

1900 Robert M. La Follette Sr. is elected governor of Wisconsin; Progressive Era begins.

1929 The Great Depression begins.

1946 Joseph McCarthy wins U.S. Senate election; McCarthy Era begins.

1967 & 1968 The Green Bay Packers win the first two Super Bowls.

1986 Tommy Thompson is elected governor.

1996 Wisconsin Works, a welfare-to-work program, is approved.

2001 Governor Tommy Thompson becomes secretary of the U.S. Department of Health and Human Services.

OUTSTANDING WISCONSINITES

Black Hawk

Ezekiel Gillespie

Marguerite Henry

Woody Herman

Black Hawk (1767–1838) was a Sauk Indian leader who tried to stop white settlers from taking over lands in Wisconsin and Illinois. In 1832 the U.S. Army defeated him in the Battle of Bad Axe, during the Black Hawk War.

Zona Gale (1874–1938) was born in Portage, Wisconsin. As a writer, Gale supported women's rights, progressive political ideas, and racial equality. She was awarded the Pulitzer Prize in drama in 1921, when her novel *Miss Lulu Bett* was performed as a play.

Ezekiel Gillespie (1818–1892) was probably born a slave. By 1852 he was living in Milwaukee. Gillespie helped win the right to vote for blacks in Wisconsin. He also helped found the first African Methodist Episcopal Church in Milwaukee.

Eric Heiden (born 1958) is considered one of the best speed skaters ever. At the 1980 Winter Olympics in Lake Placid, New York, he won four gold medals and set a world record in the 10,000-meter race. Heiden was born in Madison.

Marguerite Henry (1902–1997), originally from Milwaukee, was the author of *Misty of Chincoteague, Justin Morgan Had a Horse, King of the Wind,* and other classic children's stories about life with horses.

Woodrow ("Woody") Herman (1913–1987), originally from Milwaukee, was a leading jazz musician and bandleader during the "big band" days of the 1930s and 1940s. He was noted for his clarinet, saxophone, and vocal skills.

Harry Houdini (1874–1926) was born Erich Weiss in Hungary. A magician who grew up in Appleton, Wisconsin, Houdini was one of the most accomplished escape artists of all time. He also starred in many silent films.

Harry Houdini

Robert M. La Follette Sr. (1855–1925) was born in Primrose, Wisconsin. Nicknamed Fighting Bob, La Follette founded the Progressive political party in 1904. He served as governor of Wisconsin from 1901 to 1905 and as U.S. senator from 1906 to 1925. As the Progressive Party candidate for U.S. president in 1924, La Follette won 17 percent of the nation's vote.

Robert M. La Follette Sr.

Earl "Curly" Lambeau (1898–1965) was a professional football coach. As the founder and coach of the Green Bay Packers, Lambeau helped start the National Football League (NFL) in 1921. He was head coach of the Packers from 1919 until 1949. Lambeau was born in Green Bay.

Curly Lambeau

Wladziu Valentino Liberace (1919–1987) was born in West Allis, Wisconsin. A pianist who performed on television and on stages across the country, Liberace played showy versions of classical and modern music.

Wladziu Liberace

Vince Lombardi (1913–1970) coached the Green Bay Packers from 1959 to 1968. During this time, the professional football team won five NFL titles and the first two Super Bowl contests.

Joseph McCarthy

Joseph McCarthy (1908–1957) was born in Grand Chute, Wisconsin. As a U.S. senator from 1947 to 1957, McCarthy attacked people he thought were suspicious in any way by calling them Communists. McCarthy's wide accusations and harsh methods have come to be known as "McCarthyism."

John Muir (1838–1914), born in Scotland, spent part of his youth in Marquette County, Wisconsin. A naturalist and explorer, Muir helped establish the Sierra Club and the national park system.

Oshkosh

Jean Nicolet (1598–1642) was a French explorer. In 1634 Nicolet became the first European known to have seen Lake Michigan. He explored Green Bay, the Fox River, and most of the Wisconsin River.

Georgia O'Keeffe (1887–1986), born in Sun Prairie, Wisconsin, was one of the nation's best-known artists. She is remembered best for her series of close-up paintings of flowers, skulls, deserts, and crosses.

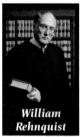

William Rehnquist

Oshkosh (1795–1858), a Menominee Indian, led his people in a successful attempt to keep their tribal lands in Wisconsin. As a result of his efforts, the federal government granted the first Menominee reservation. The city of Oshkosh is named after him.

William Rehnquist (born 1924) grew up in Shorewood, Wisconsin. He has been Chief Justice of the Supreme Court of the United States since 1986. He is known for his conservative opinions and decisions.

Spencer Tracy

Spencer Tracy (1900–1967) was born in Milwaukee. Tracy won Academy Awards as best actor in the films *Captains Courageous* and *Boys Town*.

Bob Uecker (born 1935) grew up in Milwaukee. After a short career in major league baseball, he returned to Milwaukee and became an announcer at Milwaukee Brewers games. He has starred in the television series *Mr. Belvedere* and several movies. He is also a sportscaster on network television.

Orson Welles (1915–1985), born in Kenosha, was a noted actor and director. He worked in film and radio. He is best known for *War of the Worlds*, a radio drama about a Martian invasion, and *Citizen Kane*, which is considered to be one of the best films of all time.

Orson Welles

Gene Wilder (born 1935), known as Jerry Silberman in his hometown of Milwaukee, is a comedian and actor whose films include *Young Frankenstein* and *Willy Wonka and the Chocolate Factory*.

Gene Wilder

Laura Ingalls Wilder (1867–1957), born in Pepin, Wisconsin, wrote *Little House on the Prairie* and other stories about her childhood. Her books were adapted into a long-running television series.

Thornton Wilder (1897–1975) was a writer born in Madison. He wrote novels and plays. His novel *The Bridge of San Luis Rey* won a Pulitzer Prize in 1927, and his popular play, *Our Town*, won a Pulitzer Prize in 1938.

Laura Ingalls Wilder

Frank Lloyd Wright (1867–1959) was a world-famous architect. Born in Richland Center, Wisconsin, he designed houses and other buildings to blend into the surrounding landscape, often using materials found in the area.

Frank Lloyd Wright

FACTS-AT-A-GLANCE

Nickname: Badger State

Song: "On, Wisconsin"

Motto: Forward

Flower: wood violet

Tree: sugar maple

Bird: robin

Fish: muskellunge (muskie)

Insect: honeybee

Domestic animal: dairy cow

Rock: red granite

Date and ranking of statehood: May 29, 1848, the 30th state

Capital: Madison

Area: 54,314 square miles

Rank in area, nationwide: 25th

Average January temperature: 14° F

Average July temperature: 70° F

Wisconsin's flag features symbols of some of the state's important industries: agriculture, mining, manufacturing, and navigation. The state motto, "Forward," and the state animal, the badger, also appear on the flag.

POPULATION GROWTH

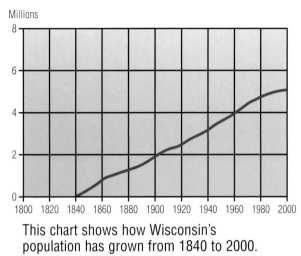

Millions

This chart shows how Wisconsin's population has grown from 1840 to 2000.

On Wisconsin's state seal, a farmer and a miner hold a shield. The shield shows symbols of Wisconsin and its economy. The seal, adopted in 1881, appears on the state flag.

Population: 5,363,675 (2000 census)

Rank in population, nationwide: 18th

Major cities and populations: (2000 census) Milwaukee (596,974), Madison (208,054), Green Bay (102,313), Kenosha (90,352), Racine (81,855)

U.S. senators: 2

U.S. representatives: 8

Electoral votes: 10

Natural resources: basalt, clay, copper, fertile soil, forests, iron, lakes and rivers, lead, peat, sand and gravel, sandstone, sulfide, zinc

Agricultural products: apples, barley, beef cattle, beets, chickens, cranberries, green peas, hay, hogs, milk, oats, potatoes, snap beans, soybeans, sweet corn, tart cherries, turkeys, wheat

Manufactured goods: electrical equipment, food products, machinery, metal products, paper products, transportation equipment

WHERE WISCONSINITES WORK

Services—60 percent (services includes jobs in trade; community, social, and personal services; finance, insurance, and real estate; transportation, communication, and utilities)

Manufacturing—19 percent

Government—12 percent

Construction—5 percent

Agriculture and fishing—4 percent

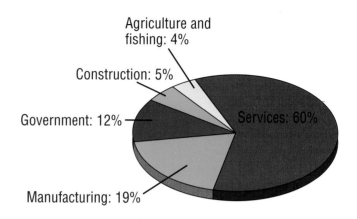

Agriculture and fishing: 4%
Construction: 5%
Government: 12%
Services: 60%
Manufacturing: 19%

GROSS STATE PRODUCT

Services—55 percent

Manufacturing—27 percent

Government—11 percent

Construction—5 percent

Agriculture and fishing—2 percent

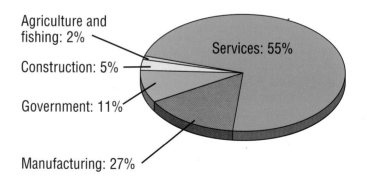

Agriculture and fishing: 2%
Construction: 5%
Government: 11%
Services: 55%
Manufacturing: 27%

WISCONSIN WILDLIFE

Mammals: badger, bear, beaver, chipmunk, coyote, deer, fox, gopher, muskrat, porcupine, prairie mouse, raccoon, woodchuck

Birds: bittern, black tern, chickadee, coot, duck, goose, jacksnipe, loon, nuthatch, partridge, pheasant, robin, ruffed grouse, snipe, swallow, warbler, woodcock, wren

Amphibians and reptiles: bullfrog, bullsnake, garter snake, newts, painted turtle, salamander, snapping turtle, toads, tree frog

Fish: bass, muskellunge, pickerel, pike, sturgeon, trout

Trees: ash, aspen, balsam fir, basswood, beech, elm, hemlock, maple, oak, pine, spruce, tamarack, white cedar, yellow birch

Wild plants: aster, blueberry, fireweed, goldenrod, huckleberry, Juneberry, trailing arbutus, violets, wild black currant

Robins' eggs

PLACES TO VISIT

Apostle Islands National Lakeshore, offshore from Bayfield
These islands in Lake Superior are covered by forests and populated by many kinds of wildlife. Visitors can camp, sail, hike, and fish.

Cave of the Mounds, between Mount Horeb and Blue Mounds
Hundreds of colorful stone formations have been shaped in these underground caverns. The cave is open for tours year-round.

Circus World Museum, Baraboo
The original headquarters of the Ringling Brothers Circus, the museum displays circus artifacts and equipment. During the summer, visitors can see circus performances.

Door County, Door Peninsula
Door County is one of Wisconsin's most popular vacation destinations. Its small towns and natural areas offer shopping, hiking, camping, backpacking, and swimming and sailing on Lake Michigan.

EAA Air Adventure Museum, Oshkosh
The Experimental Aircraft Association's museum displays many kinds of airplanes, new and old, and offers information about the history of aviation. Hundreds of thousands of visitors come to the EAA International Fly-In Convention in July and August.

Green Bay Packer Hall of Fame, Green Bay

Tackle football history at this museum. Visitors can learn about the history of the Packers and their players, from their first Super Bowl win to the current season.

House on the Rock, near Dodgeville

This unique 22-room house sits on top of a huge rock and features six fireplaces, seven pools, antiques, and the world's largest carousel.

Old World Wisconsin, near Eagle

The outdoor museum is made up of structures built by Wisconsin immigrants of the 1800s and features re-creations of pioneer life.

Milwaukee Public Museum

This museum houses one of the country's largest natural history collections. Walk through a rain forest, the streets of Old Milwaukee, or a dinosaur landscape.

Wisconsin Dells

The Wisconsin River created rock formations, known as the Dells, as it cut through the sandstone in this region. Tourists come for the natural beauty, as well as the water parks and souvenir shops in the town of Wisconsin Dells.

Door County

ANNUAL EVENTS

American Birkebeiner, Hayward—*February*

Farmers Market, Madison—*April–October*

Door County Festival of Blossoms, Door County—*May*

Walleye Weekend, Fond du Lac—*June*

Lumberjack World Championships, Hayward—*July*

Summerfest, Milwaukee—*June–July*

Great Circus Parade, Milwaukee—*July*

Hamburger Day Festival, Seymour—*August*

Experimental Aircraft Association Fly-In Convention, Oshkosh—
   July–August

Oktoberfest, La Crosse—*October*

Holiday Folk Fair, Milwaukee—*November*

LEARN MORE ABOUT WISCONSIN

BOOKS

General

Blashfield, Jean F. *Wisconsin*. New York: Children's Press, 1998. For older readers.

Fradin, Dennis Brindell. *Wisconsin*. Chicago: Children's Press, 1994.

Zeinert, Karen. *Wisconsin*. New York: Benchmark Books, 1998. For older readers.

Special Interest

Kent, Zachary. *Jacques Marquette and Louis Jolliet*. Chicago: Children's Press, 1994. For older readers. Examines the lives of Father Jacques Marquette and Louis Jolliet and their exploration of Wisconsin and the Mississippi River.

Krull, Kathleen. *One Nation, Many Tribes: How Kids Live in Milwaukee's Indian Community.* New York: Lodestar Books, 1995. Introduces Thirza Defoe and Shawnee Ford, students at Milwaukee Indian Community School. There, they explore their Native American heritage and culture.

McDaniel, Melissa. *The Sac and Fox Indians*. New York: Chelsea House Publishers, 1995. McDaniel introduces the history and way of life of the Sac and Fox Indians, and tells the story of the Black Hawk War.

Wukovits, John. *Vince Lombardi.* Philadelphia: Chelsea House Publishers, 1997. Follows one of Wisconsin's favorite football heroes throughout his career, from his humble origins in Brooklyn, New York, to his leading the Packers to two Super Bowl triumphs.

Fiction

Brink, Carol Ryrie. *Caddie Woodlawn.* New York: Simon & Schuster, 1983. The author describes the adventures of her grandmother, Caddie, who was a tomboy growing up on the Wisconsin frontier in the 1860s. First published in 1935.

Erdrich, Louise. *The Birchbark House.* New York: Hyperion Books for Children, 1999. Omakayas is a seven-year-old Ojibway girl who lives on Madeline Island in Lake Superior in 1847. Readers learn about the daily life of Omakayas and her people, and what happens during an outbreak of smallpox.

North, Sterling. *Rascal.* New York: E. P. Dutton, 1984. The author, who grew up in rural Wisconsin around the time of World War I, recalls his adventures with his pet raccoon, Rascal.

Wilder, Laura Ingalls. *Little House in the Big Woods.* New York: HarperTrophy, 1971. In the first Little House book, originally published in 1932, Laura and her family face the hardships and joys of Wisconsin pioneer life in the late 1800s.

WEBSITES

State of Wisconsin Information Server
<http://www.state.wi.us/>
Known as the "Badger," this website is a source of information
about Wisconsin state agencies, departments, and services.

Wisconsin Department of Tourism
<http://tourism.state.wi.us>
Find out what there is to see and do in Wisconsin. This site also
provides facts about Wisconsin's annual events and tourist
destinations.

**The Wisconsin Page: A Guide to Information about Wisconsin
on the Internet**
<http://www.uwsp.edu/geo/wisconsin/>
Find links to sites about Wisconsin's government, education
system, environment, and more.

Milwaukee Journal Sentinel Online
<http://www.jsonline.com/>
Read Milwaukee's major daily newspaper on the Internet.

PRONUNCIATION GUIDE

La Follette (lah FAHL-et)

Menominee (muh-NAH-muh-nee)

Milwaukee (mihl-WAU-kee)

Mississippi (mihs-uh-SIHP-ee)

Jean Nicolet (zhawn nee-koh-LAY)

Ojibway (oh-JIHB-way)

Peshtigo (PESH-tih-goh)

Potawatomi (paht-uh-WHAT-uh-mee)

Progressivism (pruh-GRESS-ihv-ihzm)

Racine (ruh-SEEN)

Saint Croix (saynt KRAWee)

voyageur (voy-eh-ZHER)

Winnebago (wihn-nuh-BAY-goh)

A Milwaukee Bucks play-off game

GLOSSARY

bluff: a steep, high bank, found especially along a river; a cliff

Communist: a person who believes in Communism, a system of government in which the state (rather than private individuals) owns and controls all farms, factories, and businesses

glacier: a large body of ice that moves slowly over land

governor: the person elected to be head of a state in the United States

groundwater: water that lies beneath the earth's surface. The water comes from rain and snow that seep through soil into the cracks and other openings in rocks. Groundwater supplies wells and springs.

ice age: a time when glaciers covered a large part of the earth. The term *Ice Age* usually refers to the most recent one, called the Pleistocene, which began almost 2 million years ago and ended about 10,000 years ago.

immigrant: a person who moves into a foreign country and settles there

missionary: a person sent out by a religious group to spread its beliefs to other people

moraine: a mass of sand, gravel, or rocks that is pushed along or left by a glacier

Progressivism: a political movement that favors new ideas and change in government in order to improve the conditions in which people live and work

reservation: public land set aside by the government to be used by Native Americans

senator: a member of the Senate, which is one of the two elected groups that make laws for the United States

treaty: an agreement between two or more groups, usually having to do with peace or trade

INDEX

PHOTO ACKNOWLEDGMENTS

Cover photographs by Tom Bean/CORBIS (left), AFP/CORBIS (right). Digital Cartographics, pp. 1, 8, 9, 46; Richard Hamilton Smith/CORBIS, pp. 2–3, 6, 43; Philip Gould/CORBIS, p. 3 (right); Janda Thompson, pp. 4 (detail), 7 (detail, left), 17 (detail, left), 39 (detail, left), 47, 51 (detail, left), 73; Milwaukee DCD, pp. 7 (right), 40; Minneapolis Public Library and Information Center, pp. 10, 51 (right); Wisconsin Department of Natural Resources, pp. 11, 15, 16 (left), 49 (left), 52; Harriet Vander Meer, pp. 12, 17 (right), 37; Olive Glasgow, pp. 13, 16 (right), 53; Green Bay Area Visitor & Convention Bureau, pp. 14, 50; Royal Ontario Museum, Toronto, Canada, p. 19; State Historical Society of Wisconsin, pp. 20, 22, 26, 30, 33, 34, 35, 67 (second from top), 68 (top, second from top); American Museum of Natural History, p. 21; French Embassy Press & Information Division, p. 23; Picture Division, Public Archives Canada, Ottawa, p. 24; Independent Picture Service, pp. 27, 67 (top); Library of Congress, pp. 28, 60; Historical Pictures Service, Chicago, pp. 32; Cy White, PHOTO ACTION USA, p. 39 (right); Yvonne & Charles Coushman, p. 41; AFP/CORBIS, pp. 42, 80; Wisconsin Paper Council, p. 44; Miller Brewing Company, p. 45 (left); Wisconsin Division of Tourism, pp. 48, 49 (right); Bryan Liedahl, p. 54; A.B. Sheldon, p. 55; Jerry Boucher, p. 56; Fotographia, Inc./CORBIS, p. 57; Walter C. Gorham, p. 58; Jack Lindstrom, p. 61; Tim Seeley, pp. 63, 71, 72; Milwaukee Co. Historical Society, p. 66 (top, second from top); Marguerite Henry, p. 66 (second from bottom); Hollywood Book and Poster Co., pp. 66 (bottom), 67 (bottom), 68 (bottom), 69 (second from top); Green Bay Press Gazette, p. 67 (second from bottom); Wally McNamee/CORBIS, p. 68 (second from bottom); Colita/CORBIS, p. 69 (top); Laura Ingalls Wilder Memorial Society, p. 69 (second from bottom); The Frank Lloyd Wright Home and Studio Foundation, p. 69 (bottom); Jean Matheny, p. 70; Eugene G. Schulz, p. 75.